Late Kate

Suzanne I. Barchers

Consultants

Robert C. Calfee, Ph.D.
Stanford University

P. David Pearson, Ph.D.
University of California, Berkeley

Publishing Credits

Dona Herweck Rice, *Editor-in-Chief*
Lee Aucoin, *Creative Director*
Sharon Coan, M.S.Ed., *Project Manager*
Jamey Acosta, *Editor*
Robin Erickson, *Designer*
Cathie Lowmiller, *Illustrator*
Robin Demougeot, *Associate Art Director*
Heather Marr, *Copy Editor*
Rachelle Cracchiolo, M.S.Ed., *Publisher*

Teacher Created Materials

5301 Oceanus Drive
Huntington Beach, CA 92649-1030
http://www.tcmpub.com

ISBN 978-1-4333-2906-7

© 2012 by Teacher Created Materials, Inc.
Printed in China WAI002

My name is Kate.
I hate to be late.

I race to make first base.

I stop to fix my lace.

I race to bake a cake.

I stop to wave at Jake.

I race to win a game.

I stop to see who came.

I race to get to the lake.

I stop for dates to take.

I race to rake and rake.

I stop to take a break.

My name is Kate.
I will not be late!

Decodable Words

and	fix	lake	stop
at	game	late	take
bake	get	make	wave
base	hate	name	will
cake	Jake	not	win
came	Kate	race	
dates	lace	rake	

Sight Words

a	my
be	see
first	the
for	to
I	who
is	

Challenge Word

break

Extension Activities

Discussion Questions

- Why does Kate stop when running to first base? *(She stops to fix her lace.)*

- Why does Kate stop when she is playing a game? *(She stops to see who came.)*

- Do you think Kate really hates to be late? Why or why not?

- Do you think Kate will be late in the future? Why or why not?

Exploring the Story

- Discuss the words *base*, *hate*, *Kate*, *lace*, *late*, and *race*. Write them out so you can see how they are spelled. Notice that all the words have a silent *e* at the end. Find other words in the story with the same pattern *(bake, cake, Jake, game, came, lake, take,* and *rake)*. Discuss how the letter *a* has the long vowel sound as heard at the beginning of the word *ape*.

- Write the following phrases on small sheets of paper: *make first base*, *bake a cake*, *win a game*, *get to the lake*, *rake and rake*. Place the papers in a sack. Use additional paper to write the following phrases: *fix a lace*, *wave at Jake*, *see who came*, *dates to take*, and *take a break*. Place these papers in a second sack. Each player takes one paper from the first sack and reads the phrase. Then he or she takes a paper from the second sack and reads the phrase. If the phrases match what happened in the story, the player keeps the match. For example, if a player draws *make first base* and *fix a lace*, that is a match. If the player does not have a match, he or she returns the papers to the sack and the next player takes a turn. The game ends when all matches are made.
Note: You may need to help read the phrases.